Presented To:

_____

By:

_____

Date:

_____

ACKNOWLEDGEMENTS

We gratefully recognize
the work of:
Illustration Elements & Chickypooh By:
The JC Collection
Cora Artz, Editor
Copyright ©2016 by Jacqueline
Charmane
The JC Collection
www.chickypooh.com

ISBN: 978-0-9974496-1-7

Wake up! wake up, said Mrs.
Young to her daughter so polite. It's
time to open your sleepy eyes. Don't
you see the morning light?

The sun is shining, the birds are
singing, and it's a beautiful brand
new day. God keep us from
temptation and harm this I daily
pray.

Samone slowly rolled to the side, pulling the covers over her head. Mommy, I didn't sleep well. Today, may I stay in bed?

I don't feel right, she complained. May I please sleep at least another hour? My stomach hurts. I think last night I must have ate something sour.

Sour? repeated Mrs. Young. You did eat hardy, which was strange. You consumed three helpings of dinner as if your appetite had changed.

Over-eating may be the reason for what you say is wrong. Then again, it could be lack of sleep. You did stay up texting your friend way too long.

And I know you're not suggesting that my cooking made you sick. Don't you know when I was young I played that same old trick?

I'd hold my stomach while bent over as I moaned and groaned. My mother would say, you must be ill then she'd hurry to the phone.

Who are you calling mommy, I'd inquire so sincere. I wanted to ensure it wasn't a place I fear.

I knew I couldn't go to the hospital, doctor, or urgent center. They'd know I was faking as soon as the very door I'd entered.

My mother would dial with haste then say doctor, please give me a cure. What I need it for? Well, as to that I am not quite sure.

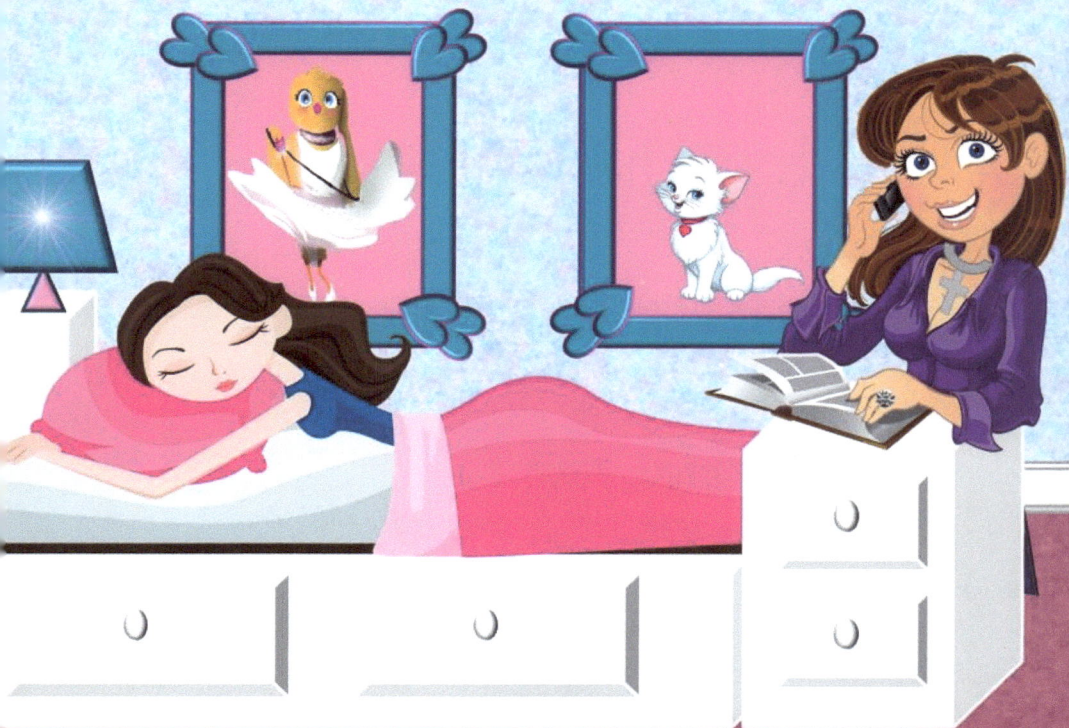

My daughter thinks I'm not aware of the games children sometimes play. For some odd reason, she seems to believe my brain is made out of clay.

From time to time, she tries to mold me based on her desire. At this rate, if she keeps it up, her punishment will become dire.

5

"Okay, thank you so much," she'd say. "Your recommendation sounds good. I'll give her a big dose or two. It should work much better than food."

A dose or two of what? I'd ask my mother, as she marched to her bedroom. My face would turn solemn as I thought about my doom.

She'd come back to my room with the Holy Bible in her hand. She'd open it up and tell me God knows all of your secret plans.

Scripture after scripture she would tell me there isn't anything God doesn't know. She'd tell me to trust in Him. That's the only way you'll grow.

Dear daughter, said Mrs. Young, I'm not like my mom. She was patient and understanding. But, right now, I don't have time to be calm.

Your grandma was a housewife. Unfortunately, I don't have that perk. I need to get you off to school so that I can go to work.

So, you have until the count of three to get up from that bed. The only way you can lay there is if you're really sick or dead.

Because your lips are moving and your voice sounds very clear. I'm sure you'll be just fine so get yourself in gear.

One, two, and three, I'm sure you know what comes next. Get up now or I'll take your phone so you can't text.

Enough of this you lazy bones. Get up and take your bath. You think you can skip because you didn't study for that test in math.

I can see your textbook still lying on your bedroom floor. You haven't picked it up since you walked through the door.

I didn't study for math, Samone said because my head ached bad. I didn't tell you about my test for the fear you would be mad.

Mommy, please forgive me for all
those times I lied. But this time I
do feel ill, Samone said as she cried.
Okay let's assume for a moment,
say I believe how you're feeling. I
hope and pray it's something that's
swift in healing.

You said your tummy hurts. Your head aches and you didn't sleep well. Is there anything else unusual that you can tell?

For the last two days, Samone wept, I've been tired with throbbing pains in my back. Each step I take feels as though I'm carrying a heavy sack.

Also, at school, I went to the bathroom and had a scare. There was a spot in my panties but I was too embarrassed to share.

Oh no! Forgive me Samone. How could I've been so blind? You're twelve now. I should've kept that fact in mind.

What does my age have to do with this? Samone asked in tears. Does this mean I won't get better until I turn another year?

Mrs. Young smiled at first then realized Samone looked so sad. Gently she said, I guarantee it will take longer than that, especially if you ask your dad.

Ask my dad? cried Samone. I
wouldn't dare say a word to him.
Can't you help me mom? Is the
situation really that grim?

It's not grim. It's more of a bother, every month for five to seven days. Thanks to Eve, it's a woman's issue that takes about forty years to go away.

Forty years! cried Samone. That's a lifetime. By then I'll be old and gray. Please say you're joking, Mommy. I can't take this for that long! NO WAY!

I'm afraid you'll have to come to grips with this, my dear, for it's the truth. But you'll learn to get used to it as a twelve-year-old youth.

Every female has to come to understand these facts and their worth. There's a beautiful side you'll experience once you wed, called the miracle of birth.

I believe it's best to introduce to you a special character known as Chickypooh. She can help you understand what you're experiencing as well as what to do.

Hi Samone. I'm Chickypooh. I'm the chick with a leash on her kitty. Don't be alarmed. This happens to females in every city.

There's much I need to tell you about but first let's start at the beginning. I'm sure by the time we're done you'll feel like your head is spinning.

Your condition has a name, but no doubt you'll hear slang works too. Just remember it's a part of life and you'll know what to do.

Doctors gave your condition the term "Menstruation" (men-STRAY-shuhn) which is its medical name. Most often you'll hear it called your "Period" which merely means the same.

Your period is a way for nature to prepare your body for a new healthy life. You'll understand the necessity of a period after you become a wife.

Until then, there're things you must do to manage your period with ease. Getting to know what they are will make each monthly cycle a breeze.

I have a kit that I prepared with things that you'll need. Included in it is a book about your body that you must read.

It's best for you to stay home today so you and your mom can shop for more. Let's buy a supply of everything to keep in a special dresser drawer.

CYCLE

SUNDAY	MONDAY	TUESDAY	WEDNESDAY	THURSDAY	FRIDAY	SATURDAY
				1	2	3
4	5	6	7	8	9	10
11	12	13	14	15	16	17
18	19	20	21	22	23	24
25	26	27	28	29	30	31

I'll show you how to keep a calendar of days when your cycle will flow. It'll also help you to know when you need to restock as your supplies get low.

Chickypooh, I thank you. The book made it easy to grasp in such a short time. What helped a lot is the way you take the facts and turn them into a rhyme.

Samone and her mom went shopping at the store in the middle of town. Being prepared by getting what she needed really help Samone to calm down.

By the time they got home she had forgotten about her trouble. But as they walked into her room, a strange odor busted her bubble.

PU! What's that smell? Samone said plugging her nose. It smells like the church's annual fish fry. Then she sniffed at her clothes.

She lifted all the windows and sprayed disinfectant from wall to wall. She even took the can of spray and fumigated the hall.

Calm down said Chickypooh. I believe I know what's that smell. You're encountering one of the most important lessons. So, please listen very well.

Each month during your period it's important that your nose is keen. You and every piece of clothing you wear must be kept extremely clean.

Don't leave soiled napkins in the trash can in your room. Everything should go into the outside garbage so that it won't leave a fume.

Your underwear must be soaked and immediately washed by hand. If there's a stain that can't come out, throw your soiled underwear in the trash can.

A stain may indicate that you're not changing your protection as often as you require. By not doing so, you may have an accident and need to change all of your attire.

Good personal hygiene is essential for you to maintain each and every day. Wash your body thoroughly before you put on deodorant and body spray.

If an odor from your body reaches your nose, remember that others can smell it, too. If you're bathing daily, but you still hear, "PU!" What's that smell? Here's what you do.

MATH EXAM TODAY

Talk to a doctor to ensure there's nothing medically wrong. A doctor can prescribe what you need so the odor will soon be gone.

The key is to know your body, no matter what's the season. That way you can better protect yourself regardless of the reason.

Don't forget about these special intimate times we've shared. Keep them in your mind and heart through high school, college and everywhere.

I'm Chickypooh, the chick with a leash on her kitty. Follow me and, read my books as I tour from city to city.

I'm here to teach you how to protect yourself and abstain, which means resisting anything improper. Don't do it. Refrain!

I'll leave you with a Chickypooh message to keep in mind as you mature. A positive attitude towards life's challenges will help bring about the best cure.

About the Author

Evangelist Jacqueline Charmane is an extremely talented and gifted woman. In 1995, Jacqueline began volunteering nationally and internationally for theatrical productions. It was through freely giving of her time that her talents in theatrical productions and cultural art were cultivated. For nearly twenty years, Jacqueline has written, directed, and performed in stage plays, as well as designed spectacular costumes and dance wardrobes. As Jacqueline worked in theater, her zeal for life and laughter unfolded.

In 1998, Jacqueline began performing gospel comedy that after a decade gave rise to the character "Mother Maeye."Jacqueline (as Mother May-eye") has been seen on *Black Entertainment Television's* (BET) website, over a dozen commercials for the famous gospel talent show *"Sunday Best"* , and has two live DVD recordings. As an author, Jacqueline has written and published eight books and has plans for more. In 2010, Jacqueline branched further out in theater by founding The JC Drama Ministries and has written three plays to date. One thing is for sure, Jacqueline Charmane wisely and uniquely uses her God-given talents.

SPECIAL ACKNOWLEDGEMENTS

Illustration Characters' Contributors:
monicabc@123rf.com
kakigori @123rf.com
Iulia Brovchenko@123rf.com
Greatnotions@123rf.com
Lorelyn Medina @123rf.com
Igor Zakowski @123rf.com
Summersun@123rf.com
Eric Blak@christart.com
Digitalart@365fact.com
Biblestudyclipart@clipartoons.com

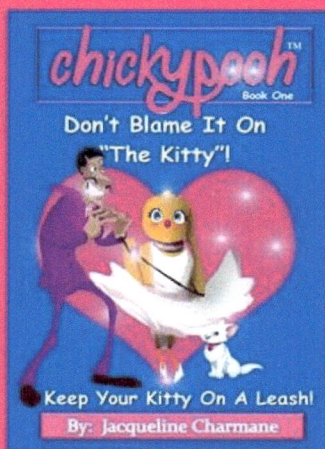

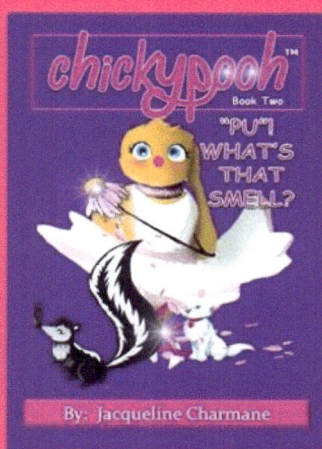

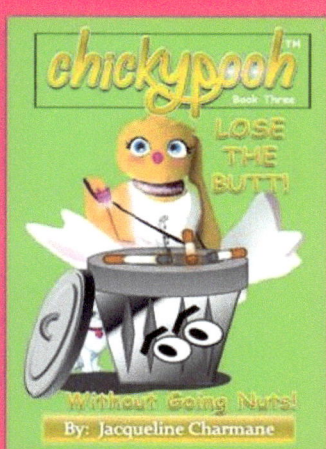

www.ingramcontent.com/pod-product-compliance
Lightning Source LLC
Chambersburg PA
CBHW041804040426
42448CB00001B/34